Introducti‹

DOLGELLAU, at the head of the magi is an ideal centre for exploring the of the Snowdonia National Park. Al are located close to Dolgellau, with their star 25 minute drive away from the town by car, anu an are in scenery that is remarkably varied and interesting. There are paths on high ridges, in open moorland and nature reserves, along rivers, lakes or the estuary, near waterfalls, following old mining tracks and among moss-cushioned boulders in woodlands of oak, beech, ash and birch. This new expanded edition now contains 20 walks, and includes another fine summit, stunning views and ancient forests.

Any of these walks can be undertaken by a reasonably fit person, with **Walks 12** & **20** being the most challenging. Walking boots or strong shoes are recommended for all walks except **17**, and *please* bear in mind that this is sheep farming country – dogs must be kept on a lead at all times (or left behind).

Walk 17, Tal y Waen, can be undertaken by wheelchair users accompanied by their helpers, and offers splendid views.

The location of each walk is shown on the back cover and a summary of the key characteristics of each is given. An estimated time is also given, but for those who enjoy fine views, and are likely to linger over them, it is best to allow longer.

Each walk has a map and description which enables it to be followed without further help, but always take account of the weather, and dress accordingly, *especially if you are exploring the higher routes*. Also, take time to explore the town of Dolgellau and visit the Tourist Information Centre on Eldon Square, the shops and the pubs & hotels.

About the authors Geoff Elliott & Märit Olsson

Geoff Elliott was born in Cardiff. He worked at the Government's Welsh Office where duties often meant travel throughout Wales. Always a very keen walker, it soon became clear to him that Merionnydd (as was) had a greater variety of beautiful natural landscapes than any other county in Wales. After taking early retirement he came to live in the area he found so appealing, to explore it more deeply and introduce it to others.

Märit Olsson grew up in the north of Sweden and moved to Gwynedd in her early twenties. She has explored the local countryside extensively and enjoys finding new routes which give visitors a great experience of what she considers to be one of the most beautiful places in the world.

WALK I
GANLLWYD-DOLMELYNLLYN

DESCRIPTION A 3 mile walk with only moderate ascents, through beautiful woodlands and visiting a spectacular waterfall. It passes the site of former gold mining operations and gives extensive views over the Coed-y-Brenin Forest. Allow 2 hours.

START Car park and riverside picnic area at Ganllwyd. SH 727243.

DIRECTIONS From Dolgellau take the A470 north-west towards Betws-y-Coed. After 5 miles, just after entering the village of Ganllwyd, the car park is on the RIGHT.

Leave the car park close by the National Trust information board and cross the road. Go a short distance LEFT and then turn RIGHT up a narrow surfaced road alongside the village hall, going through a road gate. *The Afon Gamlan is on the left, tumbling over boulders and rocks.* Within about 200 yards, where the road forks, keep LEFT, continuing uphill. After about the same distance and at the second bend to the right, take a path off LEFT to reach a National Trust waymark post visible 20 yards ahead. At the post turn LEFT through the oak trees and moss covered boulders along a path towards the river. After 50 yards there is another waymark post indicating the path down to the river and a footbridge. IGNORE this and instead continue straight ahead to a stone tablet close to a fence. *The tablet contains lines from a poem by Thomas Gray and is relatively new. The original inscription can just be made out on the stone to the left of the new tablet.* Go down to the footbridge, cross the river *(look out for heron and dippers)* and turn RIGHT along the rough path to view the falls. *Their name, Rhaeadr Ddu (the Black Falls) derives from the dark rocks over which the Gamlan plunges into two slightly separated high falls.* Follow the rough path to above the upper fall and carry on for about another 50 yards to a waymark post. As indicated, go LEFT into the wood along a narrow path. When a wall is reached go LEFT continuing on the same path, which runs roughly parallel to the wall on the right. *Look out for deer in this beautiful wood.*

2 Within about 300 yards a waymark post and ladder stile are reached. *Ignore the signed post* and turn RIGHT to cross the stile over the wall. Then turn LEFT along a well defined but slightly overgrown path. Eventually, at conifer trees, a rough surfaced forest road is reached. Go across it and along a wide track to another waymark post 40 yards ahead. Follow half-LEFT in the direction indicated, along the same wide track in the wood. *An old partly collapsed wall is reached, many of its stones covered in thick moss – on the other side of this is a stream rushing down from the crags ahead – Y Garn.* Keep along this track to reach another waymark post close to a wide forest road. Stay on the track, as indicated, going straight ahead to a stile in the wall on the left, about 40 yards further on.

3 Push down and step over this interestingly designed stile and cross the footbridge. *The buildings ahead on the open hillside are all relics of the period 1862 to 1914, when gold was being sought here. This was the Cefn Coch mine, the third richest in the Meirionnydd gold belt, which stretched along the north side of the Mawddach Estuary, from near Barmouth to close to Llanelltyd, and then roughly north almost to Trawsfynydd.* Go half-RIGHT along the laid stone pathway over boggy ground and up through the small boulders to the waymark post at the wide track ahead. Go LEFT up to the buildings. *Nearby are the settling ponds, parts of the tramway, and the barracks where some of the miners lived. To the east there are fine views across the Coed y Brenin Forest to Rhobell Fawr and the Arenig Mountains. To the west is the escarpment shouldering the north-east side of Y Garn.* Carry on along the wide track, passing to the right of the ruins of the barracks, and gradually getting closer to the stone wall on the left. Soon a ladder stile over the wall is reached: cross the wall and follow the waymarked path down through the bracken until another ladder stile over the next wall is reached. Cross this, and make for the small ruined building half-RIGHT ahead. Pass to the left of the building and proceed down to a gate seen in the fence 75 yards ahead. Cross the fence by the stile near the gate and across the road to go half-LEFT down to a footbridge and gate in 100 yards.

4 Go through the gate and turn RIGHT, taking the path with a wall on the right into the wood. At the next waymark by the wall,

keep straight on, continuing down along the path through the wood until, near the edge of the wood, a fence and a low sign post are reached. Go through the gate in the fence and down to a stone wall. Go LEFT along the wall. Soon after the wall goes sharply right, cross to the stile in the fence ahead. *The Afon Gamlan is now nearby on the left.* Carry on down to the gap in the wall ahead next to a small slate-roofed outbuilding and out through a gate onto the main road. The car park is 100 yards to the left.

COED Y BRENIN & THE AFON MAWDDACH

DESCRIPTION A new bridge allows the choice of a 2½ mile or 3½ mile easy walk through mixed woodland, in a beautiful deep narrow valley seldom far from the sound of the Afon Mawddach, as it tumbles along its rocky bed. Two waterfalls and the site of one of the area's principal former gold mines are visited. Allow 1½ – 2 hours. Coed-y-brenin is now a popular mountain-biking centre, so look out for cyclists
START At a forest picnic site about 6 miles north of Dolgellau. SH 735263

DIRECTIONS Take the A470 north-west from Dolgellau in the direction of Betws y Coed. After about 5 miles the village of Ganllwyd is reached. Go through the village to the far (northern) end and, close to the traffic speed derestriction signs, turn RIGHT along a minor road. Cross the bridge over the river and go RIGHT. Pass the first car park on the right and continue for about a mile to park at the forest picnic site Tyddyn Gwladys.

I Leave the picnic area alongside the Afon Mawddach and go RIGHT along the road and on to a roughly surfaced forest track. Go through a gate and continue ahead until the house *Ferndale* is reached. Pass by the road barrier to the left of the property and carry on along the road. *The derelict remains of buildings hereabouts amongst the trees are ruins from past mining activities, mainly lead and gold.* Soon after the road and river bend to the left, the first of the two water-falls can be seen through the trees across to the right. *This is the Rhaeadr Mawddach, situated just up the river from where another river, the Afon Cain, joins the Mawddach.* Continue along the road, which goes further left and then swings right to a bridge over the Afon Cain.

2 *At the bridge the second falls – Pystyll Cain – can be seen higher up the ravine to the left.* At the far end of the bridge there is a rough narrow track to the LEFT which goes closer to the falls, and from which their full height can be seen. *This is a beautiful ravine at any time, but a visit after heavy rainfall will be especially memorable.* Return to the bridge and turn LEFT to continue along the forest road. *A short distance along to the right are the remains of the buildings associated with the Gwynfynydd gold mine where gold was first found in 1864. There was a large processing mill here but it was destroyed by fire in 1935.* Continue along the road, now rising and curving to the left. Near the top of the slope *Rhaeadr Mawddach* can be seen below on the right. *The difference between the Welsh words used to name these waterfalls will now be clear: 'pistyll' where the fall, on the Cain, is narrow and spout-like; 'rhaeadr' where the fall, on the Mawddach, is much wider.* In another 150 yards there is a stone bridge across the Afon Mawddach.

3 Cross the bridge and follow the road around to the right and uphill. Where it levels out, and at a white-top post numbered 19, go RIGHT along another forest road. *The rivers are now well below on the right and soon, where the trees have been cleared, both waterfalls can be seen.* Carry on along the road and when it forks, at a white-top post numbered 20, go RIGHT. Continue with the Mawddach generally close and below on the right and cross the first bridge for the shorter walk. An attractive path leads back to the picnic site. For the longer walk, stay on the road until a second high bridge across the river is reached. There is another white-top post here, numbered 51.

4 Cross the bridge and go up to the sur-faced minor road. Go RIGHT to return to the picnic site.

Waterfalls ③

Afon Cain ②

Afon Mawddach

former mill

Afon Mawddach

Ferndale G

N

START ① G P

F.B.

Afon Mawddach

to Ganllwyd ④ F.B.

0 ¼ mile

There are other attractive river valleys in Coed y Brenin (the King's Forest) and many more tracks and footpaths which can be explored. In 2006 a new Forest Visitor Centre opened which is signed off the A470 about 2 miles north of Ganllwyd. It is an interesting building and has a café which is open seven days a week all year round. Well worth visiting.

How the buildings at the Gwynfynydd gold mine once looked, where new machinery was installed during a revival of enthusiasm for Welsh gold in the 1930s.
These buildings were almost totally destroyed by fire in February 1935.

WALK 3
LLANFACHRETH

DESCRIPTION An moderate 4½ mile walk crossing varied terrain but mainly in open, very quiet and beautiful countryside with extensive views. An initial steady climb brings you to an elevated section which can, at certain times after rainfall, be quite wet – you will have to cross small streams. And be sure to follow the instructions carefully at point 4. Allow 4 hours.

START Parking area alongside Llanfachreth Village School. SH 756225. Toilets are available on the village side of the school.

DIRECTIONS Go north out of Dolgellau town centre and across the Afon Wnion bridge. Turn RIGHT in front of the Council Offices. After ⅓ mile turn LEFT along the minor road signed 'Precipice Walk' and 'Llanfachreth'. After 2 miles go past the car park for the Precipice Walk (see **Walk 5**) and continue straight on to Llanfachreth. At the village turn RIGHT to go past the church and reach the school. The parking area is on the left, just beyond the school.

1 Leave the parking area and turn RIGHT along the road, passing in front of the school. Turn RIGHT again at the side of the school, taking the signed path. Look for a gate ahead and go through it and along a wide grassy track with a fence on the left. Continue up this track until the fence on the left ends, follow a footpath marker turning RIGHT through the opening to turn immediately LEFT along the wall to follow the track ahead now with the wall on your left. IGNORE the footpath sign on the right, keep walking straight ahead and go into the trees by a footpath marker to reach a gate into a conifer wood.

2 Go through the gate and follow a wide path to reach another gate slightly to the right. Go through this gate and half-LEFT into an open field and along a faint track roughly parallel to the wall and fence on the left. At the end of the field go through another gate at a shallow stream crossing. Carry on ahead along the track, with the stream on the left. The path soon leaves the

stream and rises gently into open ground. Follow it to the left, to be walking parallel to, but slightly away from, an old partly broken wall on the left (not visible when bracken is high). *On the right there are some fine views of the foothills of Rhobell Fawr.* The path drops down to go through the wall. Keep on ahead to go through the gap in another stone wall. Carry on, keeping close to the fence and wall on the left, to reach a waymarked and slightly concealed gate ahead.

3 Go through the gate and follow the faint track through the rock outcrops, keeping roughly parallel to the fence on the right. Cross a small stream and continue along the rising track which now veers slightly left, away from the wall on the right, and passes to the right of some large rocky outcrops ahead. This grassy track soon joins a rough surfaced road which comes in from below on the right. Carry on ahead along this road. *There are extensive views back to Cadair Idris and the Dyfi Forest.* Go through a gate and over the pass, Bwlch Goriwared. *Once through the pass there are fine views ahead across Coed y Brenin and beyond.* Go through another gate, and the track drops down to join a forest road. Turn LEFT and go slightly uphill for about 100 yards to a waymark post on the left. Go LEFT here, following the narrow path up through the trees to reach, at the top, a stone wall and gate.

4 Go through the gate into an open area of heather and moorland grass. Carry on straight ahead along a narrow path at the bottom of a sloping heather-covered bank on the right. Continue along this path for about 200 yards to where it divides at a small heap of stones. Go half-LEFT through the heather along another narrow path, aiming just to the left of a prominent, heather covered, rocky knoll. At the far end of the knoll, carry on in the same direction, going gently uphill, and again following just to the left of another sloping, heather-covered, rocky bank. Continue in the same direction (NOT half-right) passing between two sloping banks of heather to reach the top of the rise. *Here there are extensive views to the right (west) across Coed y Brenin to the*

Rhinogydd, south-west to Y Garn, and straight ahead to Foel Offrwm (in the foreground) and Cadair Idris beyond.

5 At the wall ahead go through the gap, and immediately drop down half-RIGHT to the bottom of the small valley. Turn LEFT along the grassy track towards a wall ahead. At the wall go half-RIGHT alongside it. *Llyn Cynwch and the Precipice Walk (see Walk 5) are now visible ahead with, just a little further to the right, Bryniau Glo (see Walk 8) prominent on the far side of the Mawddach Valley.* Continue on down along the track near the wall. *Even more extensive views open up, this time to the left, to the Arans.* The track passes the ruins of a former farm-house on the left, and then soon after a gate reaches a surfaced road alongside an occupied property, *Tyn y Mynydd.* Follow the road down, through two gates, to Llanfachreth. At the crossroads turn LEFT to the school and the parking area.

Waymark post

white-topped post '45'

④

small pile of stones

N

⑤

G

⑤

G

G

ruined building

Tyn y Mynydd

G

G

G

③

G

G

G

②

0   ¼

mile

LLANFACHRETH

G G

Ⓟ ① START

School

Toilets

to
Dolgellau

WALK 4
MOEL CORS-Y-GARNEDD

DESCRIPTION A moderate 5¾ mile walk where you will experience the wild Mid Wales, walking through unspoiled countryside with extensive mountain views of Cadair Idris, Arran Fawddwy, the Rhinogs and more. Allow 4 – 4½ hours allowing for stops to admire the view.

START Car park next to Llanfachreth village school SH 746212.

DIRECTIONS From Dolgellau go north across Wnion bridge. Turn right in front of the council offices. After ⅓ mile turn LEFT along a minor road signed 'Precipice Walk' and 'Llanfachreth'. After 2 miles go past the car park for Precipice walk (see **Walk 7**) and continue straight on to Llanfachreth. At the village turn RIGHT to go past the church and reach the school. The parking area is on the left, just beyond the school.

I Leave the parking area and turn RIGHT. After the school, before the bridge, turn RIGHT onto a signed footpath to shortly go through a gate. Follow a wide grassy track with a wall on your right. When you get to a gateway on your right, follow a footpath marker turning RIGHT through the opening to turn immediately LEFT to follow the track ahead now with the wall on your left. Just before the wall ends turn RIGHT along a marked footpath and through a small gate. Follow the track ahead with the fence on your left. Coming up towards a house the track bends to the RIGHT along a fence to cross a stile. Turn LEFT to follow the track. At the end of the track turn half RIGHT up to a telegraph pole in front of you. Go downhill and through a small gate ahead of you. Turn half-RIGHT and walk to a footpath marker in the middle of the field, carry on half-RIGHT up to a stile. Cross the stile to meet a road. Turn RIGHT and follow the road down over a bridge and up to a T junction. Cross the road and take a track slightly to the RIGHT going up by a footpath marker. Follow the track as it bends left and by the next footpath marker turn LEFT to follow the grass track, cross a

stile in the fence slightly right in front of you. Carry on uphill straight ahead to another footpath marker and turn RIGHT. *On your right you will now be able to see the Precipice Walk and Foel Offrwm.*

2 Go through a gate to walk with the wall on your right. Cross a ladder stile in front of you, carry on straight ahead. When reach-

ing two ladder stiles cross over the RIGHT stile and follow the path with the wall now on your left. Passing a small cottage on the left, join a track and soon a tarmac road. Turn LEFT to follow the road. *You will now be able to see Cadair Idris to the right followed by Waun-Oer and Glascwm.* Follow this road through four gates and at the T junction turn LEFT to follow the road. *You will gradually see more of the mountains as you carry on uphill. On a clear day you should be able to see Aran Fawddwy.*

3 After four gates you will see the remains of a mine in the fields around you. Look out for a footpath sign on your left just before a small ruined building. *This is Cae'r Defaid Slate Mine. The mine operated in the late 19th to the early 20thC. You are at the upper level which was developed first but failed to prosper. There is a small mine shaft slightly to the right of the building and what is left of the tramways on the right of you.* Turn left by the footpath sign to follow the path diagonally left up the hill to a wall. Ignore the stile ahead of you and turn LEFT to follow the wall to a stile in the corner.

Moel Cors-
Y garnedd

Caer Defaid
slate mine

landmark
only

N

0   ¼
mile

4 Cross the stile and follow the path to get to a yellow topped pole straight ahead of you. Carry on along the path, passing marker posts as you are going along, until you meet the wall. Turn left along the wall and carry on to a ladder stile. Cross the ladder stile. Follow the path ahead. It very soon bends half-LEFT to go across the mound ahead and continues to the left corner of the field. Go through a gap in the wall. Look for a large rock/outcrop ahead of you. Follow the path as it bends down to the right of this rock, then passing a small hawthorn on your right and soon another on your left. *Looking half-right you can now see the Rhinogs. First Y Lletr, a rounded col, Rhinog Fach, a sharp*

col and then Rhinog Fawr. Turn RIGHT by a footpath marker and follow the path. Turn LEFT along a faint path to walk to the left of some large stones (about 15 yards before the wall). Follow the path passing footpath markers and alongside a house down to a track. Turn LEFT along the track and then RIGHT by a footpath marker to follow the path down the slope. Go through a gap in the wall to join another track. Turn RIGHT and follow this track through a gate to meet a tarmac road. Turn LEFT along the road. By a signpost with four footpath signs turn RIGHT on to the road to Cea Glas. You now re-join your outward route, to return to start.

WALK 5
PRECIPICE WALK

DESCRIPTION A very popular and easy to follow 4 mile walk. There are outstanding views over the Mawddach valley and estuary, Coed y Brenin Forest, and the Cadair Idris range. There are no steep gradients. Allow 2 hours, although you are likely to want to stay longer.

START A National Park car park specifically for the walk will be found at the start. SH 746212.

DIRECTIONS Go north out of Dolgellau over the Afon Wnion bridge and turn RIGHT in front of the Council offices. After ⅓ mile turn LEFT along the minor road signed 'Llanfachreth' and 'Precipice Walk'. The car park is 2 miles further along on your left.

1 From the car park turn LEFT along the road signed 'Hermon', and after about 100 yards go LEFT again on a rough surfaced track into a wood. Within about 200 yards, at the end of the wood, follow the track RIGHT and, when a cottage is reached, go LEFT. *There is a view to your left here of Nannau Hall, built in 1693 and until the 1960s the home of the Vaughan family, the large land-owners in this area. Most of the cottages hereabouts belonged to the estate: their often unusually high and elaborate chimneys are a feature of the estate architecture.* Climb the ladder stile ahead and turn RIGHT. Follow this path as it curves to the left and on to climb another ladder stile. Go straight ahead to the footpath sign near the end of the wall on your right.

2 Follow the direction of the sign along the wall around to the RIGHT, go over a ladder stile and keep ahead on the clear path with the wall still on your right. *There are extensive views over the wall towards the village of Llanfachreth (see Walks 3 & 4) and its church, set below the hill Rhobell Fawr: further to the right in the far distance are the Aran mountains, the highest in Meirionnydd at 2970 feet, while sharp right, and much closer, is Foel Offrwm, topped by an Iron Age hill fort.* As the path leaves the wall and curves around to the left, *the undulating wooded slopes of the Coed y Brenin Forest (the King's Forest) are seen and, if the air is clear, some of the higher mountains of northern Snowdonia.* Continuing along the path and after climbing a ladder stile, you are soon high above the Afon Mawddach. *On the opposite side of the valley (where part of Walk 6 can be seen) are the lower slopes and upper open grassland of Y Garn. The Mawddach Estuary and the sea beyond Barmouth gradually come into view.* Climb another ladder stile and soon the whole of the Cadair Idris range and its magnificent northern escarpment are visible directly ahead. Continue along the path and, at about the next ladder stile, *Dolgellau can be seen in the valley between you and Cadair Idris. (If you go RIGHT just before the ladder stile there is a memorial seat at a fine viewpoint).* Climb the ladder stile and the path gradually bears left, away from the estuary, and reaches another ladder stile.

3 Climb the stile and Llyn Cynwch comes into view. Follow the path straight ahead to reach the shore. Turn sharp LEFT here along the shore and continue along the tree lined path which keeps close to the lake. *At the end of the lake look back over it and to Cadair Idris far beyond; a view to cherish.* The path now rejoins the outward route and can be retraced back to the car park.

to
Llanfachreth

START

to
Dolgellau

Mawddach Valley

Llyn Cynwch

Memorial
seat

N

0 ——————— 1/4
mile

Nannau Hall

WALK 6

COED GARTH GELL RESERVE

DESCRIPTION An easy 3½ mile walk, mainly in the beautiful deciduous woodlands of an RSPB reserve, with spectacular views of the Afon Mawddach estuary. Buzzards, ravens, dippers and wagtails are seen all year, and there are many visiting summer birds. The walk is on the gold-mining belt which runs along the north side of the Mawddach estuary: there are interesting industrial remains. Allow 2½ hours.

START National Park car park and picnic site at Fiddler's Elbow, a short distance east of Bontddu, on the A496 about 5 miles from Dolgellau. SH 678189.

DIRECTIONS From Dolgellau go north-west along the A470 towards Betws-y-Coed. After 2 miles, at the roundabout at Llanelltyd, go LEFT along the A496 towards Barmouth. The lay-by car park and picnic area is about 3 miles along on the right, just before Bontddu village.

I From the car park go up the footpath-signed wide driveway amongst the trees. Stay on this lane, going very sharp RIGHT where it makes a turn at the top of the hill. The lane climbs again but soon levels out. Go through the gate ahead into the grounds of a modern dwelling, *Penygribin*. It is a private drive, but a public right of way. Keep on the driveway towards the house, then go LEFT under an archway at the end of the building. Keep left across the garden grass and go LEFT along the narrow track waymarked on a tree ahead. Go over a stile in the fence ahead and continue along the path through the trees. Soon cross another stile and carry on until a wall and fence are reached. Go straight ahead along the narrow path between the wall and the fence. Continue close to the wall until a wall across the path is reached. Step over it at its lowest point to enter the Reserve. There is an RSPB board on the left and a small stone structure on the right.

2 Carry on until a ruined building on the right is reached. Immediately after this there is a gap in the wall ahead. Go through it and continue ahead, passing to the right of the remains of another building almost smothered in creeper. Soon the path goes downhill to join a wide track. Go RIGHT, downhill to an RSPB information board. Go LEFT along the path indicated by a blue waymark, alongside a fence on the right. The path soon goes through an old gateway and enters Cwm Mynach, the monks' valley. *The river below on the right is Afon Cwmmynach, and the track is a former tramway, used in the 19th century in connection with mining operations. Before that it might well also have been one of the routes used by the monks of Cymer Abbey, just north of Dolgellau, who owned land here and whose advanced farming practices would have encouraged tree clearance and sheep breeding in the upper, broader sections of this valley. Whatever its history it is a beautiful path to walk now. After about ⅓ mile the site of a former mill is reached. The interesting six round structures low down near the river are the foundations of buddles, used in the process of separating out the metal ores.*

3 Carry on along the track up the valley to reach the old smithy. Go straight head passing to the right of the building. *The path now becomes more open, allowing views of the hills across the valley on the right.* Keep on the path as it curves LEFT and away from the river. It soon curves around to the RIGHT and reaches a gate and ladder stile over a wall. Ignore the route to the left. Leave the Reserve by the ladder-stile and head along the wide track leading from it. It curves slightly right and passes to the right of the top of a small knoll ahead, climbing slightly. After passing the knoll and its few trees, the broad path is in an open area *giving fine views ahead and across to the other side of Cwm Mynach.* Keep on this path up to a gate in the wall ahead. DO NOT GO THROUGH, but turn sharp LEFT keeping in the same field. Continue up to the corner of the field and turn LEFT again, keeping parallel to the wall, and then a fence, on the right. At the end of the field, and a little way down the wall from the corner, is a gate.

4 Go through and enter the reserve again. Carry on along the path. It eventually drops down through a gap in a low stone wall. Continue ahead along the winding path through the trees, passing a bench. *It is on this section that there are the finest views, to the left and slightly back, of the hills on the other side of Cwm Mynach, reaching to the summit of Y Garn.* Keep ahead on the obvious path, through another old wall, and reaching a substantial wall with a sign indicating to go through the gap in it. There is another bench here. *Further down there are fine views of the whole of the Cadair Idris range and, below, of the hamlet of Penmaenpool (**Walk 10**) on the other side of the Afon Mawddach, but linked to this side by the wooden toll bridge.* Continue along and go through yet another gap. When past a gorse and heather covered knoll ahead, *even more spectacular views open up: the rough tops of Pared y Cefn-hir (**Walk 14**) further down the Mawddach, and on to the mouth of the estuary at Barmouth. There is a conveniently placed bench a little ahead, from which the views extend to the Aran Mountains in the extreme east and around to the sea in the west.* The path continues down into the trees.

Afon Cwm-mynach

Landmark→ only, do not go through

④

Coed Garth-gell

Old Smithy

③

Old mine buildings

N

⑤ old cottage (remains)

Landmark only

② RSPB board

START

to Bontddu

P

A

①

Penygribin

old building (remains)

0 ¼ mile

A496 ← to Dolgellau

5 At the bottom of the dell another sign indicates a path to the left. *Do NOT take this* but go RIGHT along a broad path towards a stone wall. Continue ahead alongside the wall to a gate ahead. Go through and continue ahead with the wall on the left. Soon there is a gate in this wall: carry on past it until another similar gate is reached. Go through this gate out on to the lane and turn RIGHT, to the car park.

WALK 7
NEW PRECIPICE WALK

DESCRIPTION A moderate 4 mile walk with outstanding views from an old industrial tramway 800 feet above the Mawddach Estuary. The path climbs steadily and fairly steeply from the start, but with a rest possible at an attractive lake set in the hills. After the tramway, which offers stupendous views over the Mawddach estuary, the path drops through both deciduous and evergreen trees. *Rare breed pigs roam freely in the woods at the start of this walk – they are sometimes curious, but very soon lose interest in you.* **Do not attempt to feed them or approach their off-spring. If you have a dog with you, keep it on a lead and close by you.** Allow 3 hours.

START Park by a section of the old road off the present A496. SH 707196.

DIRECTIONS From Dolgellau go north-west along the A470 towards Betws-y-coed. After 2 miles, at the Llanelltyd roundabout, turn LEFT along the A496 towards Barmouth. Look for the speed derestriction signs about ½ mile along this road. Just beyond them the road bends to the left and then to the right. Immediately after the bend to the right, SLOW DOWN and look for the gated entrance to a now disused section of the old main road. Turn RIGHT to park opposite the gate.

I Go through the gate onto the old section of road, and turn RIGHT through a kissing gate on the right. Follow the green and white waymarks uphill. After about 20 yards veer LEFT to cross a stream on stones. Turn RIGHT to continue uphill on a path which zig-zags and climbs steeply, passing a gate on the left and looking for a stile AHEAD. Cross this and continue uphill with a fence on the right. Pass fenced-off mine shafts to the left and continue. Cross stile on the RIGHT and now continue with the fence to your left. Cross a ladder stile and turn RIGHt to cross a bridge. Turn right and follow a faint path through conifers to reach a little clearing, with stones in the ground. Walk ahead a few yards then turn LEFT uphill through trees on a rough path, keeping a stream in a gully

over to your right. Soon you pass the top of the gully and the path becomes clear and distinct. When the path splits at a waymark post fork RIGHT to continue to Llyn Tan-y-graig.

2 At a T-junction turn RIGHT to visit Llyn Tan-y-graig. Return from the lake on this track, continuing ahead and uphill to a path junction with a waymark post, Walk half-LEFT uphill along a clear path through a less dense area of pine trees, with steeply sloping ground down to the left. *There are soon glimpses of the panoramic views to come.* The path eventually reaches a ladder stile in a wall ahead.

3 Go over the ladder stile and turn LEFT alongside the wall. Pass to the right of the ruined house ahead and up a slope ato-cross the footbridge over the stream. Carry on ahead, parallel to the wall and passing another ruined building. After about another 100 yards the path leaves the wall on the left and goes uphill to a gap in the wall ahead. DO NOT go up the much steeper path going further to the right, which is part of an old tramway incline. *This is the end of climbing and the start of the magnificent views from the 'precipice' along the side of Foel Ispri. Ahead, westwards, is the beautiful Mawddach Estuary, completely covered at high tide, and at other times displaying winding silver ribbons reaching to the sea at Barmouth. To the south is the whole length of the Cadair Idris ridge and the undulating landscape between it and the Mawddach. The hamlet below, at the end of the wooden bridge, is Penmaenpool (see* **Walk 10**). *Far to the east are the Aran Mountains. The path now follows an old level tramway used in the last half of the nineteenth century to transport zinc and lead ore to a mill in Cwm-mynach (see* **Walk 6**). Carry on along the tramway, eventually going through a swing gate and passing in front of and below an occupied house, *Foel Ispri Uchaf.*

4 Just beyond the house – *which has a fine ruined waterwheel amongst the out-buildings* – there is a gate at the start of a surfaced road. Do NOT go through this but turn back sharp LEFT down a wide green track through a gateway to a waymarked

```
                                    ③        Llyn
                    F.B.        S       Tan-y-graig
surfaced  Landmark only
road  G Foel Ispri Uchaf      ruins    ②
  ④ G
N    G    G                          ①
                                    — old road
                                  P START
                                    A496 to
  ⑤ L                  A496 to    Dolgellau
                       Barmouth
```

```
0          ¼
      mile
```

gate. Go through and continue downhill, passing through another gate. Follow the obvious path down to reach a gate in a wall. Go through, continuing downhill. Stay on the downhill path which zig-zags through the conifer trees and eventually reaches a rough surfaced, level and slightly overgrown forestry track.

5 Ignore the waymark and turn LEFT, walking over an engraved stone in the path, to follow a narrow path in the middle of this rather overgrown track. After a little over half a mile the path becomes a wider forest track. Continue ahead along it. *You may see some pigs again around here.* Where the track ends at a fence, go LEFT a short distance along the fence and turn RIGHT over a stile into a deciduous wood, where you continue ahead and soon cross another stile, rejoining your outward route and following the white arrows back to the lay-by. The path is steep and needs care when you are descending, especially during or after wet weather.

On the approach to
the old tramway

WALK 8

AROUND BRYNIAU GLO

DESCRIPTION A moderate 5 mile walk giving dramatic near and long-distance views. The route goes through varied woodland, and with one high level superb open section. Some uphill, but not too steep, parts. Allow about 3 hours.

START National Park car park and picnic area alongside the Afon Mawddach, close to the old road bridge south of Llanelltyd. SH 719193.

DIRECTIONS Take the A470 north-west from Dolgellau towards Betws y Coed. Just outside Dolgellau, and before crossing the river bridge to Llanelltyd, turn RIGHT (east) along the minor road signed Cymer Abbey. This road reaches the old bridge in about ⅓ mile. The car park is on the right.

I Leave the car park via the entrance and turn RIGHT to cross the old bridge over the Afon Mawddach. *There is a fine view back from the bridge of the three peaks of Cadair Idris: from east to west – Mynydd Moel, Penygadair and Cyfrwy.* Immediately after the bridge go half-RIGHT along the signed footpath. At the end of the path, at some houses, go ahead up a surfaced lane to the main road. *St Illtud's Church is on the left. It dates originally from the 13th century and has many interesting features, including a now rare circular churchyard. There are helpful explanatory notes inside and a visit is worthwhile.* Cross the road and go up the steps ahead to reach a minor road. Turn RIGHT along it. Where it joins the road coming up from the village go LEFT for 30 yards, then RIGHT along a signed, roughly surfaced, wide track. After about ⅓ mile the track divides. Keep RIGHT and carry on to a stile over a fence.

2 Cross the stile and go ahead along a narrow path with a fence on the left. *The river below is the Afon Mawddach. There are soon fine views up the valley with the hill Rhobell Fawr dominating in the distance, half-right ahead. Across the valley, to the right, the path of the Precipice Walk (***Walk 5***)*

can be seen high up on Foel Cynwch. Cross the ladder stile reached at the end of the trees on the left and continue along the path ahead. Where it widens and curves right and left at a rocky knoll it is worth looking back towards Cadair Idris.

3 Carry on to reach a gate and a stile in a wall. Cross the stile and go along the path through oak trees. After about 60 yards the path curves LEFT at the edge of the trees and continues through bracken to the left of a high rocky mound and on to the corner of a low wall on the left. At the end of this short low wall go sharp LEFT again along a narrow path through the bracken, soon with an old low wall on the right. Follow the wall on the right, and in about 50 yards reach a small low rocky outcrop on the left where there is a small pile of stones. Go around the stones sharp LEFT, picking out the path through the bracken to reach another low stone wall in about 40 yards. Keep on ahead with the wall on the right, and at the wall corner in another 40 yards, follow the path just half-RIGHT where the wall itself turns sharp right. The path rises slightly and soon goes through gaps close together in two walls, probably enclosing old sheep pens. Carry on ahead with walls about 30 yards apart on either side. *There are extensive views northwards across the Coed y Brenin forest to the distant mountains of northern Snowdonia.* The path drops down to cross a small stream. After passing close to the right of some rock outcrops it is best to move slightly LEFT towards the wall on the left to reach a gate in about 100 yards. Go through, dropping down to cross another small stream, and carry on keeping close to the wall on the left. Where the wall goes half left, follow it uphill, keeping close to the wall at first but later moving away from it onto a clearer path. *When the route levels out a short diversion across the open ground on the right to above the top of the rocky outcrops will be well rewarded with magnificent views; it is the highest point on the walk.* Carry on parallel to the wall to reach a gate and stile.

4 Go through and ahead. When, in about 60 yards, the path divides, go LEFT

16

downhill. The path emerges at a forest road. Go LEFT along it and in about ½ mile reach a minor surfaced road. Go LEFT again. This valley is Cwm Wnin. *After about ¼ mile there is a signed footpath through the trees on the right. This leads to a footbridge over the Afon Wnin, and this beautiful spot is a pleasant diversion.* Returning to the road carry on along it to Llanelltyd. Just past the speed restriction signs turn RIGHT along the road used on the outward route. Near to the end of this road go LEFT down the steps to the church and the car park.

Hafod Y fedw

N

Bryniau Glo

Afon Mawddach

Afon Wnin

F.B.

0   ¼

mile

Village Houses

30mph Signs

LLANELLTYD

Steps

A470

Trem Y Gader

St Illtud's Church

Ysgoldy

Toilets

START

to Dolgellau

WALK 9
COED Y GARTH

DESCRIPTION An easy 3 mile walk through an ancient natural woodland site with stunning views over the Mawddach estuary and mountain range. The path is easy to follow and there are no steep gradients. Allow 2 hours. There are picnic areas along the route.

START A gateway next to a garage. SH 668168.

DIRECTIONS Leave Dolgellau from the top (southern) end of Eldon Square, along the road to Tywyn. After about 1 mile turn left at the T-junction towards Tywyn. After roughly 2½ miles you cross a bridge on a sharp corner by Abergwynant Farm. Ignore the first turning to the right and take the second RIGHT in front of some buildings. Park against the fence to the right or drive through the gate to park just inside.

I Walk through the gate and follow the forestry track straight ahead of you. At the crossroads turn RIGHT up the hill walking past a house and some chalets. Keep to the LEFT at the next junction. *Very soon you will have the first glimpses of the mountain range across the estuary. There is a viewpoint and picnic area signposted just up the hill to the LEFT. It is well worth making a short stop here to admire the view over the estuary and the mountain range ahead of you. You will see the top of Diffwys to the right with the mountain range sloping down on the left towards Barmouth.*

2 Coming back down to the track turn LEFT and you will very soon come to a junction. Turn RIGHT and follow the track for 300 yards to where the road splits. Keep RIGHT. You will now enter an area of old woodland with lots of different habitats for small animals. *Keeps a lookout for marked poles along the track with small information signs hidden inside them. The track turns into a narrow path following parallel with the Mawddach estuary. You can now see Barmouth bridge straight ahead and on the other side of the estuary the mountain range, with the highest peak Diffwys to the right.*

3 At the bottom of the hill the path turns to the LEFT and widens to become a track. Carry on until you reach a junction and turn RIGHT. You will very soon reach two small ponds with a picnic table. *You will find an information board here telling you about the wildlife and trees in the area.* Carry on along the track. Ignore the faint track going off to the right shortly after the ponds. At the junction turn RIGHT and walk down the lane back to the car.

The toll bridge,
Penmaenpool

18

Bontddu

N

0   ¼
mile

Afon Mawddach

← bench & viewpoint

picnic table & information board

Abergwynant Farm

Penmaenpool - Morfa Mawddach Walk

② pond

③

Coed y Garth

① G START
lake
to Dolgellau

A493

to Fairbourne

THE MAWDDACH ESTUARY AT PENMAENPOOL

DESCRIPTION A 5 mile walk with some moderate uphill sections near the start, but with outstanding views of mountains and the estuary. The route passes through varied woodland and open countryside, and finishes amidst the peace of Wales' most beautiful estuary, using the track of a disused railway. Take binoculars to see the estuarial birds. Allow 3 hours.

START At the National Park car park close to the toll bridge at Penmaenpool. SH 696185.
DIRECTIONS From Dolgellau take the A493 road to Tywyn. After about 2½ miles, just as Penmaenpool is reached, turn RIGHT at the 30 mph signs for the toll bridge road to Barmouth. About 30 yards further on turn RIGHT again into the car park.

1 Leave the car park by going past the toilet block and the RSPB Wildlife Centre, on to the narrow road in front of the hotel. Go as far as the old railway signal (about 100 yards) and take the path half LEFT up to the hotel entrance; then go sharp LEFT to the road. Turn RIGHT along the road. After 75 yards go sharp LEFT along a signed path. Continue up this winding path for about 100 yards until a gate is reached. Go through it onto a minor road. Turn LEFT along the road and when, in 200 yards, it forks, take the RIGHT fork along a roughly surfaced forestry track. Continue for about ⅓ mile until a pond is reached low down on the left, and just before the track takes a bend to the left.

2 Opposite the pond take the waymarked path half RIGHT uphill. It climbs moderately steeply. After 200 yards go over a ladder stile and continue ahead through oak trees into a flat and more open area. Look for a rough surfaced track just ahead and turn RIGHT along it. When, in about 100 yards, it divides, go RIGHT and continue

20

along it, passing to the left of a barn and reaching a ladder stile. Stay on the track, crossing another ladder stile and then going on through a gate into a farmyard. *There are fine views from this track to the Cadair Idris range far away on the left.* In the farmyard turn RIGHT taking the track alongside the stone barn and out, through a gate, into an open field.

3 Go LEFT uphill to the top of the field, aiming for a wooden post about 200 yards ahead at the top. *From near the post there are extensive views back over Dolgellau and beyond to the Aran Mountains, while to the right (south) the Cadair Idris range is again in sight.* At the post turn RIGHT along a wide track and follow this to a ladder stile

PENMAENPOOL
START
Toll Bridge ① P Toilets
George III
Hotel
to
Dolgellau

to Tywyn N

↑

0 ¼
mile

Pond
②

Barn

③

Tyn-y-llwyn

and a small shallow stream. Cross and carry on half-LEFT through a gap in an old wall into another field. Go straight ahead, keeping roughly parallel to the fence and then a wall on the left, and making for another ladder stile in a wall about 250 yards ahead. Go over and bear slightly RIGHT to keep clear of the marshy ground ahead on the left. When opposite the massive rock scree on the left

go partly RIGHT up a grass track to the top of the rise. *From here there is a fine first view of the Mawddach Estuary, but go over to the highest ground further right (north) for spectacular all-round views.* Drop down from this high ground in the general direction you were heading (west) and look for, and go over, the stone slab steps in the wall ahead. Their position is indicated by a way-marked post on the top of the wall.

4 Go RIGHT along a rough surfaced track a little ahead. *There are soon more extensive views of the estuary and Barmouth bridge and, as you continue downhill, the wooded slopes of the Gwynant valley.* Stay on this track, crossing two ladder stiles and then going through a gate onto a minor road.

5 Turn RIGHT down this road to the main Dolgellau – Tywyn road. At the main road turn LEFT but in 25 yards turn RIGHT along the narrow road signed to *Abergwynant Farm. The Afon Gwynant is now close on your left.* In about ¼ mile the road crosses the river. *Do not cross* but go straight ahead through a gate and along a surfaced track, keeping the river on your left. When some gates are reached, go through the one nearest the river (and waymarked), and on to another waymarked gate visible in the wall ahead. After this next gate go left along the track. Keep on this wide level track until an open area is reached. Do NOT follow the wide track going half-right into the wood here but go AHEAD, close to the river, and directly towards the estuary.

6 Go up to what was the railway track, turn RIGHT and keep on it for about 1¼ miles to return to the car park. *It is flat all the way back, of course, and there are fine views over the Mawddach Estuary, with an opportunity to observe the many visiting birds (as long as you have remembered to bring along your binoculars!). The railway track which once occupied this route used to carry trains from near Barmouth to Dolgellau, but it was sadly closed, like so many other rural lines, in the 1960s.*

The former signal box at Penmaenpool is now the RSPB Wildlife Centre.

WALK 11

TORRENT WALK

DESCRIPTION A popular and easy 2½ mile walk using a path close to a tumbling river in a beautiful ravine, and including the chance to visit the remains of an old charcoal blast furnace, used for smelting iron. This walk, enjoyable at all times, is at its very best after rain, when the river will be running full. The original route east of the river, which this route follows, has recently been re-opened. Allow 1½ hours.

START Lay-by on the B4416 just west of Brithdir. SH 761181.

DIRECTIONS Take the A470 east from Dolgellau towards Machynlleth. After about 2 miles turn LEFT (east) along the B4416 towards Brithdir. After crossing the narrow bridge over the river, park in the first lay-by on the left side, a distance of ½ mile from the main A470 road.

The Torrent Walk was designed and engineered by Thomas Payne, who also designed the embankment across the estuary at Porthmadog, known as The Cob. The Torrent Walk was planned as an extension of the gardens of Caerynwch house nearby, which were open to the public from their completion early in the 19th century. Thomas Payne died in Dolgellau in 1834 aged 73, and there is a memorial plate to him there in St Mary's church.

1 Walk to the wooden gate by the lay-by. Go through and follow the path between fences. Continue along the path, with the falls to your left. *The road to your right is thought to be the line of an old Roman road leading to, and beyond, a Roman fortlet at Brithdir about 1 mile to the east. You are now walking on what was the original route of the Torrent walk, and which has been recently restored. You pass through two gates and*

walk behind some beautifully constructed wooden barriers before reaching the road, where you turn LEFT.

2 Continue along to the LEFT past a group of cottages in an attractive valley-bottom setting. *These cottages were formerly a woollen mill and its associated warehouses.* After crossing the road bridge over the river – and having the first sight of the Afon Clywedog – the way into the Torrent Walk is through a gate immediately on your LEFT. However, by walking just a further 200 yards along the road and turning RIGHT into the drive of the Fronalchen caravan site, it is possible to view the remains of an early 18th century charcoal blast furnace. *These remains, a little way down the entrance drive on the right hand side, were excavated and consolidated in 1982 and 1983 by students from the Snowdonia National Park Environmental Studies Centre at Maentwrog.*

3 Return to the bridge and turn RIGHT into the Torrent Walk. For some way ahead the path remains close to and on about the same level as the river (ignore the path going up the 12 steps to the right) but it gradually climbs, eventually leaving the river well below. However, the ascent is never steep, and there are short flights of steps in places to assist the climb. *The beauty of the gorge, and the continually varying views of the Clywedog tumbling over and around the rocks and boulders in its path, make this a walk to be taken slowly. There is a seat, about two thirds of the way up the path, provided by the North Wales Wildlife Trust in memory of Mary Richards, a well known local botanist who died in 1977.*

4 At the top of the ravine cross the footbridge over the river *(constructed about 1970 to replace Thomas Payne's original crossing)* and go out through the gate ahead to the road. Turn LEFT along the road to return to the lay-by just 100 yards ahead.

After the walk try to make time for a visit to the nearby St Mark's Church. It is formally listed as a building of special architectural and historic interest, and one of the very few such buildings in Wales to be classed as Grade 1. It was the major work of Henry Wilson, one of the leading post-William Morris figures of the Arts & Crafts Movement. The interior is richly painted and contains some remarkable high quality copper furnishings. Many architectural historians consider it to be an important and advanced work for its time of completion, which was in 1898.

St Mark's Church, Brithdir

WALK 12
ARAN FAWDDWY

DESCRIPTION A challenging 7½ mile walk which takes you up a long grassy slope, along the ridge of Drws Bach with a final climb up a rocky section to bring you to the top of Arran Fawddwy (2970 ft), Wales' highest peak south of Snowdon. You will pass Creiglyn Dyfi, the source of the Afon Dyfi, and experience some breathtaking views. Your return is through craggy fields and the final descent is down a steep rocky slope. There are some wet sections. *This is a challenging walk and should not be attempted in bad weather.* Allow 7½ hours.

START Car park in Cwm Cywarch. SH 852187

DIRECTIONS From Dolgellau take the A470 towards Welshpool & Llangurig. After 9½ miles turn left where signed to Dinas Mawddwy. Keep straight ahead by the Red Lion and continue, taking the second left to Cwm Cywarch. Follow the road to the car park, which is signposted just after a footbridge. Parking is free but a donation for the Wales Air Ambulance is appreciated. There is a portaloo in the car park.

I Come out of the car park and turn RIGHT to follow the road. Shortly turn LEFT over a footbridge onto a marked footpath. Go through a kissing gate and soon another gate to follow the path straight ahead. Follow the path as it turns round to the left, ignoring the footpath sign and stile on the right. Follow the path, crossing stiles as you go. *As you walk, look at the slate stones in the path. You can clearly see how the slate is formed into layers to make natural ridges in the stone.* You soon meet a track. Turn LEFT along this track walking diagonally up the hill. After a small stream the track bends down to the left. Keep walking straight ahead, following the marked footpath to carry on walking diagonally up the slope, crossing a stile along the way. As you reach the top of the ridge where the path levels out you can see a fence in front of you. Turn LEFT to follow the path up the grassy slope with the fence on your right. At the top, cross a stile and follow the path ahead to join and walk with the fence

on your right. You are now walking along a narrow ridge to get to Drws Bach (small door). At the end of the ridge you will reach a cairn with a memorial plaque. *Stop here to take in the view of Craig Cywarch to your left, with Maesglase behind, the top of Aran Faddwy half right and Y Berwyn to your right. The small lake Creiflyn Dyfi that you see below you on the right is the source of the river Dyfi.*

2 Carry on following the path with the fence on your right. As you reach a corner of the fence cross the stile on your RIGHT to carry on straight ahead, (ignoring another stile immediately to your LEFT) follow the path up to the summit of Aran Fawddwy and the trig point. *Standing with your back to the trig point following the panorama view from Bala lake to Arenig Fawr and Moel Llyfnant in front followed by the distinctive three peaks joined together, the pointed Rhinogs Fawr, Rhinogs Fach with the flat top followed by Y Llethr with the ridge and Diffwys sloping down towards Barmouth. Crossing the estuary you will see the Cadair Idris range and much closer on your right is Glasgwm. Behind you is Y Berwyn Nature Reserve.*

3 Turn to walk towards the fence below, back the way you came. Walking with the fence on your right ignore a stile on your right and carry on along the fence until you meet a stile ahead of you. Cross the stile and carry on straight ahead, walking down hill with the fence on your right. Some sections lower down are very wet but board walks will take you through the worst parts. These boards can be very slippery in wet weather, *so please take care.* Further down you cross a stile. Keep walking with the fence on your right until you reach a flatter area where you can see Glasgwm starting to slope up in front of you. The path will bend to the LEFT between a small pond and a pole and onwards towards a fence. Just before the fence the path turns LEFT to follow the stream. Follow this steep path down towards Cwm Cwarch. This area is very steep and rocky. *Please take care as you find your way down.* The path leads down to a footbridge. Cross this and turn LEFT along a marked

Creiglyn Dyfi

Aran Fawddwy

③

② cairn

Drws Bach

Some slippery sections TAKE CARE!

N

0 — mile — ¼

Afon yr Hengwm

pond

VERY ROCKY & STEEP DESCENT!

F.B.

Glasgwm

Blaencywarch

Cwm Cywarch

① P

toilet

START → to Dinas Mawddwy

F.B.

footpath. The path turns LEFT along a wall to shortly get to a stile. Cross the stile to meet a track ahead of you, turn RIGHT along this track. Pass a farm and carry on straight ahead to a gate. After the gate walk a further 30 yards and turn RIGHT into the car park.

WALK 13
AROUND FOEL DINAS

DESCRIPTION A 5½ mile walk with breathtaking views over two valleys and a spectacularly high waterfall. You pass through varied countryside and forestry. It is a moderate to energetic walk, with two steep ascents and one steep descent. Allow 5–5½ hours, including stops to enjoy the views. The Red Lion pub offers real ale and excellent food.

START Car park in Dinas Mawddwy. (with toilets). SH 858149

DIRECTIONS Take the A470 east towards Welshpool & Llangurig. After 9½ miles turn left into Dinas Mawddwy village. The car park is on the left by the public toilets.

1 Leaving the car park turn left down the hill. Follow the road until you cross a bridge, then turn left into the access road to a caravan park. Turn immediately right along a marked footpath and through a gate. Follow the path and after a small wooded area turn half-RIGHT across the field to a small gate at the top of the field. Turn LEFT and follow the lane through a gate and down onto a tarmac road. Follow the road as it bends to the left and crosses a bridge to a T junction. Turn left and carry on up to the main road (A470). Turn RIGHT, cross the road and take the next road on the LEFT.

2 Follow the road, passing through a gate by a farm and continuing uphill. As the road ascends turn LEFT through a gate by a small memorial, on to a marked footpath. *The memorial tells us that the remnants of the home of Hugh Jones, the hymnist, are not far from here. He was born in Maesglase but spent some time teaching in London before returning. Between 1798 to 1817 he taught in the area and from 1817 he worked as a translator, translating books for publication. He was also a musician and composed hymns such as 'Capel Cynon' He died 16 April 1825.* Follow the track through a gate and up to a small wooded area. *Look to the right as you walk up the track to see a very high waterfall*

coming down the side of Maesglase. Climb the stile at the edge of the woods and carry on past some ruined buildings. *Along here on your left you can see a second waterfall.* Follow the path as it climbs diagonally up the steep side of Blwch Siglen aiming for where the two hills meet. As you come up the hill you will see a fence in front of you with forestry growing behind. Turn LEFT to meet the fence and you will shortly see a stile and some waymarks. *Stop to admire the view of the valley behind you, Maesglase to the leftt and the top of Aran Fawddwy just peaking out from behind the mountain in front of you.*

3 Cross the stile. Follow the path straight ahead down the hill to shortly turn LEFT by the waymark. Follow the path diagonally down the hill towards the road. Cross the road to carry on down a marked footpath on the RIGHT. Keep a lookout for a marked footpath to the left going up the bank. Follow this path until you are level with the stream on your right. Now look out for a waymark and a stile on the opposite side of the stream. Cross over the stile and turn LEFT. (There are no stepping stones in the stream so in wet weather this can be difficult to pass.)

4 Cross the stile next to a gate and follow the track half-RIGHT up the hill. The path will curve around the hill and as you come further up the hill aim for the lowest point where the two hills meet. *Reaching the top of the ridge you might like to go off the route slightly to a higher point to admire the view. Behind you is the Dyfi Forest, to your left the view of Foel Dinas and*

Maesglase in the background. Looking above the mountain to your left you can see the top of Aran Fawddwy and in front of you the valley of Dinas Mawddwy.

5 You will now start your descent. Carry on straight ahead down the hill and keep to the right as the quarry comes into view. Follow the slope down to the middle of the upper level of the quarry. Turn right down a steep incline. *As you reach the bottom of the quarry look to the left behind you to see the ornate stone-lined mine tunnel on the left. The Minllyn slate quarry was in use from the mid 1800s and was finally closed in 1925. It started*

as an open hillside quarry but expanded the workings underground in the 1870s. Typical annual tonnage was 550 tons, and it employed around 50 men.

6 Carry on through the quarry meeting a fence. Keep to the LEFT of the fence, to reach a stone stile. Cross the stile and turn LEFT following a track into the forest. Follow the path down the hill, crossing a forestry road, down to the main road A470. Cross the A470 and turn LEFT to take the first turning to the RIGHT into the village. You will soon see the car park in front of you.

WALK 14
LLYNNAU CREGENNEN

DESCRIPTION A mainly level 5½ mile walk in an area many people consider to be the most beautiful in Meirionnydd. There are fine views of the dominating northern escarpment of Cadair Idris for much of the walk, which also includes a superb riverside path in the wooded Afon Gwynant valley. Allow 3–4 hours (it is too scenic to rush!).

START Car park (with toilets) at Cregennen Lakes. SH 658142.

DIRECTIONS Leave Dolgellau from the top (southern) end of Eldon Square along the road to Tywyn. After about ½ mile take the minor road half-LEFT signed 'Cadair Idris'. Go about 4½ miles and then take the road signed 'Cregennen Lakes' to the RIGHT. The car park is ¾ mile along this road, on the left.

1 Leave the car park and go LEFT along the road for about 300 yards to reach a waymark post. *Look left here for a view down to the Mawddach Estuary. The land across the horizon is the Llyn Peninsula.* Go sharp RIGHT across open ground to a ladder stile over a wall.

2 Cross the stile and take the path half-RIGHT through the heather. (*The path half-left takes you to the top of the steep hill – Pared y Cefn-hir – if you are feeling energetic. There are fine views from the top and it is possible to walk along the ridge and drop down at the end of the walk near point 3 at Ty'n Llidiart*). Continue along the path (ignoring the waymark sign to the right soon after passing the lake) and reach a high, but partly broken, stone wall on the right. The path continues roughly

parallel to the wall. After a while it goes slightly uphill, over a brief boggy area, and then soon drops down close to the wall. *There are views to your right to the Craig-las escarpment, at about 2200 feet.* Soon the path curves left and runs alongside a wall at right angles to the one followed so far. Continue along the path as it drops down and turns RIGHT downhill to a gate and ladder stile in the wall ahead.

3 Go over the stile and then half-RIGHT across a field to a gap in a wall, about 50 yards ahead. Continue through this gap and go half-LEFT to reach a another gap in the wall 100 yards ahead. Go through and carry on parallel, and soon close, to a low wall on the right. The path becomes a farm vehicle track. Keep along it and, where it divides, keep RIGHT towards a small group of trees, and then on to a gate ahead. Go through the gate and keep on the track, until a surfaced road is reached. Go LEFT along the road for about 200 yards, with the stream dropping lower into a ravine on the right, to a ruined chapel on the left, *where the cemetery is still used.*

4 At the cemetery gates go RIGHT along a wide path into a wood and follow this down until a

28

gate is reached. Go through and up to a sur-faced road. Turn RIGHT downhill, and in 100 yards, at a road junction, turn RIGHT again and pass in front of a youth hostel. Cross the river at the road bridge and then immediately go RIGHT through a gate into a field with the river on your right.

5 Go across the field to a gate ahead. Pass through it and continue along the path through trees. After a while the path climbs slightly and curves LEFT alongside a fence to reach a swing gate. Go through and turn RIGHT to reach a sloping field. Keep straight ahead across the bottom of the field to a nar-row stone footbridge, surmounted by a small gate, across two streams. Pass through into another field and carry on ahead with a low wall on the right. *The river is*

below to the right and there are soon views of Cadair Idris ahead. Keep along this path. It gradually drops down close to the river and becomes a rough surfaced track. Another, but more substantial, footbridge is reached. Cross it and go ahead uphill along the rough track and through a gate at the top. Cross the track leading to the farm down on the right and carry on straight ahead along the rough track, through a gate and across to another gate in the far corner, close to farm buildings.

6 Go through the gate and turn RIGHT along a minor unclassified road. Stay on this road for about ¾ mile and, just before a cattle grid, turn off RIGHT, go through a gate and follow a rough surfaced track signed *Nantygwyrddail Farm.* Continue along it to the farm. Pass to the right of the outbuildings and cross a ladder stile alongside a gate in the wall ahead. Carry on along the slightly uphill track to reach another lad-der stile. Cross this. The larger Cregennen Lake comes into view.

7 Continue ahead along the track, which curves slightly to the right. Soon a low rocky mound appears ahead: pass to the left of it, by a low wooden way-mark post. Go down the slope ahead to another low waymark. Carry on in the direction of the lake, following a faint path with marker posts to a ladder stile in the wall ahead. Cross over the stile and follow the path ahead through the heather to the lake. Step across the small outlet stream, and at the lake edge go RIGHT for about 50 yards. Then leave the lake edge and keep ahead to the right of a small mound, staying on the main path until, in about 200 yards, the path used at the start of the walk is reached. Turn LEFT along it to return to the car park.

Kings Youth Hostel

Cemetery

④

Afon Gwynant

⑤

F.B.

N

F.B.

Ty'n-y-Ceunant (Teas)

Farm buildings

⑥

0   ¼
       mile

Cattle grid

WALK 15
BRAICH DDU

DESCRIPTION A moderate but spectacular 6½ mile walk with extensive views and the feel of mountain walking (but with much less effort!). Starting along a cycle route and passing a standing stone you walk through fields to reach the first peak of the Cadair Idris range – Braich Ddu. There are spectacular views of the Cadair Idris range as well as the Mawdach Estuary, Barmouth and Fairbourne. You return to the cycle path by a moderately steep grassy slope. Allow 5 hours to allow plenty of time to admire the views. If you feel energetic you can extend this walk and carry on further along the ridge of the Cadair range.

START A minor road junction just after the turning to Cregennen Lakes. SH 656134

DIRECTIONS Leave Dolgellau from the top (southern) end of Eldon Square along the road to Tywyn. After about ½ mile take the minor road half-left signed 'Cader Idris'. After 5 miles (shortly after the turning to Cregennen Lakes) go through a gate and park on the road-side just before the road forks by a cycle path sign.

I Follow the track up the hill to the left marked as cycle track 82. *After going through a gate you will see a standing stone on your right. Further along you will soon have views of the estuary and the mountain range behind it on your left.* After walking through another two gates, coming up towards a small mount, look to your right to see a monument on the stone wall below. *This commemorates a World War II aeroplane crash. You have beautiful views of Barmouth and the estuary at this point.*

2 Having passed one gate at the beginning of the forest which lines the right-hand side of the track go through another gate. Shortly after a small stream turn LEFT, almost back on yourself, onto a marked footpath. Follow the path as it gently bends round the hillside to eventually meet a fence in front of you. Turn LEFT to continue parallel with the fence.

3 Where three fences meet cross the stile to your RIGHT. Turn LEFT and follow the fence until you reach the corner. Turn RIGHT and walk along the fence to the next corner. Cross the stile in front of you and immediately cross the stile on the LEFT. *It is well worth turning right here to walk a bit further along the ridge of Cadair Idris. Just beyond the next field you will have stunning views of Llyn Cyri and the Cregennen Lakes in the valley below you. After having taken in the views return to the stile in the fence.*

4 Follow the path with the fence on your left. Cross a stile in front of you and carry on along the fence to the next stile. *Look behind you here to see the length of the Cadair Idris ridge to the summit.* Cross the stile and follow the path parallel with the fence. As the fence bends into a corner walk straight ahead to come away from the track by the fence slightly, to enjoy a most spectacular view. *On your right you can still see the ridge of Cadair Idris up to the summit of Penygadair. Around to the left you can see Diffwys as the highest point of the ridge across the estuary. Follow the ridge as it slopes down towards Barmouth, nestling at the end of the mountain range below you. Barmouth bridge is in full view with the railway track leading off left to Fairbourne.*

5 Return to the path and carry on with the fence on your left to start your descent. As you meet the cycle track turn RIGHT to follow the track. You are now on your outward route. *On your way back you can make a slight detour to the standing stone along a grassy path, before returning to your car.*

to Dolgellau ➤

Standing
Stone

Cycle track
82

① START

Afon Arthog

G

G

G

G

N

0   ¼

mile

viewpoint

⑤
S   S

Braich Ddu

S

Llyn
Cyri

③
S

④
S S

viewpoint

LLYN GWERNAN & AN OLD TRACKWAY

DESCRIPTION A 4 mile moderate walk in beautiful, undulating mixed scenery. Initially there are fine views of the northern escarpment of Cadair Idris and of the hills across the wooded Gwynant valley, followed by very extensive views to the far hills and mountains north and east of Dolgellau. The route partly traces an old trackway and passes close to prehistoric burial cairns and hill forts. The final section is alongside Llyn Gwernan. Allow 2½ hours.

START Snowdonia National Park car park (with toilets) and picnic area at Ty Nant, 3 miles south west of Dolgellau. SH 698152.

DIRECTIONS Leave Dolgellau town centre from the top (southern) end of Eldon Square along the road towards Tywyn. After about ½ mile go half-LEFT along the minor road signed Cadair Idris. The car park is 3 miles further along, on the right.

Leave the car park by going out on to the farm lane passing close to the right of the toilets. Turn LEFT along it, go through a gate and continue ahead along the track signed *Tyddyn Farm*. After about 100 yards, where the track divides, keep straight ahead and go through a gate. Continue along the track through two more gates to reach the farm. Keeping close to a wall on the left, go through another gate to pass close to the left of the farm buildings. Leave the farmyard area by going ahead through yet another gate and on to a grass covered track, with a fence on the left. Carry on through a gate ahead, continuing along the track. After about 50 yards go slightly RIGHT through a gap in the wall, but continue in the same general direction, now with a fence on the right and a wall on the left. *From here there are fine views back to the Cadair Idris ridge.* Go through the gate ahead into

32

a steeply sloping field. Go down the slope, as indicated by a waymark post, to a wall below. At the wall go LEFT, following it closely as it curves around to the right. The path now descends and goes through a gap in the wall ahead, becoming a wider track. It curves left, moving away from the wall and continuing fairly steeply down. Where it becomes less steep, at a waymark, go RIGHT, down to a stream and a gate.

2 Cross the stream, and go through the gate up to a farm vehicle track 10 yards ahead. Go across the track and up along a narrow path amongst the birch and oak trees. Follow this path to a gate in the fence. Go through the gate and veer LEFT, close to

Gellilwyd

derelict barn

④

Llyn Gwernan

⑤ Gwernan Lake Hotel

the fence. The path becomes a track and goes through a gate and on to a point where it divides. Take the rough stony track half RIGHT uphill. Ignore a branch to the right after 50 yards, and carry on ahead to reach a gap in a stone wall. Do not go through this gap, but continue uphill with the wall on the left until a small gate is reached. Go through it. Notice the fine barn on the left. Go through the gate ahead with 'PATH' painted on it. It leads to a track between two parallel stone walls.

3 Go through the gate and on to this track. Because of a blockage just ahead it is better for the next 50 yards to walk outside this walled track, on the left-hand side, but then dropping down on to it just past the short stone wall built across the track. Now keep along this walled track for the whole of its length of about one mile. *The origins of this old track are not clear, but it could be prehistoric, as there are a number of burial cairns close to it, as well as two Iron Age hill forts. The parallel walls suggest later use as a drove route for local hill farmers.* After walking the track for a little over ¼ mile a gate is reached. *From here the remains of a hill fort can be seen on the ridge across the valley on the right – not at the highest point but at a rocky mound about half-way down. It is named Craig y Castell on OS maps. Look also for the burial cairns shown on the map.* The end of this walled track is at a wall. Go over the stile and carry on ahead along a wide grass track, passing to the right of a high gorse-covered mound. Cross a small stream and continue down the track as it curves left and then right to reach a stile in a fence. Go over and follow the track down to a derelict farm building.

4 Turn RIGHT here along a rough stone track, soon with a fence on the left, to reach a ladder stile. Cross the stile and go half-RIGHT along the narrow path into the wooded area. Continue ahead through the trees. Follow the path to the lake edge and keep along it to the right, reaching a ladder stile over a wall, at the end of the lake.

5 Cross this stile and walk along the narrow path through trees, keeping to the right of the lake's outlet stream. Follow this path to a gap in the wall ahead. Go through the gap and follow the waymarks for a new path cut through the trees by Snowdonia National Park. The path winds somewhat but runs roughly parallel to the right-of-way and goes over three stiles. After the third stile continue ahead to join the farm track. Turn LEFT along it to go through the gate into the car park.

TAL Y WAEN

DESCRIPTION This is an easy-to-follow 3½ mile walk with fine panoramic views. It can be taken by parents with children in pushchairs, as it is entirely on surfaced but very quiet roads, which for all but a short section serve merely to give access to a few nearby farms. Any length of the walk would also be suitable for wheelchair users and their helpers. As it is in varied and always interesting countryside it is also a walk, of course, for all who enjoy fine views but do not object to walking along a quiet and little-used road.

START At a minor road junction ½ mile from Dolgellau, along the road towards the Cadair Idris car park at Ty Nant. SH 718172.

DIRECTIONS The start is just under ¾ mile

from the centre of Dolgellau: if you wish to park your car in the town, walk from the town centre along Cadair Road towards Tywyn. Then, near the edge of the town, take the minor road going half LEFT, signed 'Cadair Idris'. The start is ½ mile along this road where another minor road leads off to the right towards Bryn y Gwin farm. For those coming by car there is room at this quiet junction to park. For drivers with wheelchair-user passengers who may wish to try only a short length of this walk, follow the walk directions and park in one of the open areas alongside the road in the section with the extensive views (marked **X-Y** on the map). This is after the third cattle grid, but before the first gate across the road.

I Go along the road over the cattle grid (or through the gate) towards Bryn y Gwin Farm, through a pleasant wooded area. Keep on the road past the driveway to the farm. It soon curves to the left, and just before the next cattle grid and gate are glimpses to the

34

right of the fine views to come. Continue along the road. There is soon another grid and beyond this, after the road goes slightly left, it enters an open area with much hawthorn, gorse and bracken. *There are clear views to the right, across to the hills on the other side of the Mawddach Estuary. Directly opposite is the route of the New Precipice Walk (see **Walk 7**) and it is possible to pick out, about two-thirds up the steep slope of Foel Ispri, the horizontal line of the former mineral tramway, which is now part of that walk. The higher top immediately above Foel Ispri, but set further back, is Y Garn. To the left of Ispri, and also set back, is the high ridge running south-west from the Rhinogydd mountains to Barmouth at the mouth of the Estuary.*

2 Carry on along the road. At the top of the first rise the Cadair Idris range comes into view on the left. *The three peaks*

from left to right (east to west) are Mynydd Moel, Pen y Gadair (2928 feet) and Cyfrwy. The road now dips but then quickly rises again, and at the top of this rise are the most extensive views. *To the right, looking far back (north-east) is the village of Llanelltyd, beyond which the Afon Mawddach runs in a deep, steep sided valley. This valley is the area for two other walks: **Walk 8** – Bryniau Glo on the west side, and **Walk 5** – Precipice Walk on the east. The mountains well beyond the far end of the valley are the Arenigs. To their right, and much nearer, is the dome-shaped Rhobell Fawr, and the long high ranges set back even further right are the Arans.* Continue along the road, which now drops, and through the gate.

3 After some bends the entrance to *Maes Angharad* farm is reached. Here, at another gate, the road goes sharply left, and there is a waymarked stile on the right. The road is again in an open area, with fine views to Cadair Idris on the left. Pass through a gate, soon after which the road bends left, and reach Tal y Waen Farm. Go through another gate and carry on to some birch woodland with many moss covered boulders. Just beyond the woodland and before the next cattle grid are some high old metal structures set in a small ditch on the left, alongside a walled embankment. *Trying to decide what these were can make an interesting break in the walk! (The answer is below).*

4 The next building reached further along the road is Gellilwyd Fawr *a former farmhouse with a wagon entrance, graded roofing slates, and chimneys typical of the Dolgellau area, with projecting horizontal slate slabs to help direct rainwater away from the vulnerable area at the base of the stack. Just beyond this farm the track from the ladder stile on the right leads to Gwernan Lake (**Walk 16**).* Continue along the road, now dropping and with occasional glimpses of parts of Dolgellau in the valley ahead. When the road joins another coming in from the right from Ty Nant car park, go LEFT downhill for about 300 yards to reach the starting point.

Bryn y Gwin Farm

cattle grid

cattle grid

to Dolgellau

Park here or in town

START

N

to the Cadair Idris Ty Nant Car Park

0 ¼

mile

Answer: Old War Department rifle range target holders.

35

WALK 18
GLYN ARAN

DESCRIPTION A moderate 4 mile walk which starts in Dolgellau but soon enters the wooded Glyn Aran, where there were once many fulling mills for the woollen industry. Later, in open countryside, there are fine views over Dolgellau and of the surrounding hills. Allow 3 hours.

START From the Leisure Centre car park in Dolgellau. SH 731178.

DIRECTIONS From the town centre stay on the south side of the Afon Wnion and take the road east towards the A470 to Machynlleth. Before leaving the built up area turn LEFT along the road between the Government office building and the bus depot, going past the fire station to the Leisure Centre.

1 Leave the car park through the entrance and immediately turn RIGHT into the supermarket car park. Go through it and then RIGHT to the road bridge over the Afon Aran. DO NOT cross the bridge, but cross the main road and continue alongside the river, passing in front of an attractive terrace of stone cottages. Carry on up to the end of the road and take the narrow road ahead uphill and half-RIGHT. Go up this road, passing two houses on the right, beyond which the surfacing ends. Continue along the unsurfaced track until a road is reached, close to the residence *Frongoch.*

2 At the road go RIGHT and walk along it. *This is uphill walking, but the slower pace means greater enjoyment of this lovely wooded valley, with the Afon Aran down below on the right.* After about ⅓ mile a road (the first) joins from the left, with a gate across it, signed *Tyddyn Ednyfed and Dref Gerig.* Turn LEFT through this gate and walk along the road. After about 200 yards, at a junction, continue straight ahead up to another gate. Go through this gate and continue ahead, but, after about 60 yards turn very sharp RIGHT along a signed footpath. Keep along the obvious path ahead, crossing a small stream and going through a gap in a

substantial stone wall to reach the ruins of a former farmhouse on the left. Continue along the path, crossing two more small streams and then emerging out of the wood at a surfaced road alongside an old (1882) schoolhouse now converted into a dwelling.

3 Turn LEFT along the road, but go almost immediately RIGHT through a gate signed *Pandy Gader.* Go ahead across the field in front of the dwelling to cross a footbridge over the Afon Aran. Turn RIGHT along a track. *Ignore the signed footpath to the left after about 60 yards,* and continue down the track. About 100 yards after this first footpath sign, the track goes through a gap in a wall. Turn LEFT immediately after this gap and cross a stile over a fence and into a wood. Go ahead, keeping fairly close to the wall on the left. When an area of moss-covered stones is reached, bear RIGHT and walk roughly parallel to another wall on the left and along a narrow path through more mossy boulders. The path reaches the low remains of an old wall and a waymark post. Go ahead as indicated by the sign, soon going partly right and parallel to another wall ahead. Keep the wall on the left, and after about 75 yards the path reaches some more low remains of an old wall. Go through the gap and then half-LEFT to the waymark on a tree ahead (NOT straight ahead along the more obvious path). Carry on down to cross double stiles over a fence and a wall, to join a rough surfaced wide track. Turn RIGHT along it to reach a surfaced road.

4 Go LEFT along the road, passing *Parc Cottage* on the right. *This cottage was the home of the last person to be hanged in Dolgellau, Cadwaladr Jones, who confessed in 1877 to the murder of a young local woman.* Carry on along the road and, after going through a gate, passing the next house on the right, *Esgeiriau. The track opposite this property leads to Bryn Mawr, which was the home of Rowland Ellis, who became a prominent Quaker in the 17th century, and who led emigrants to the USA to escape persecution. He named his new settlement in Pennsylvania, Bryn Mawr, and the name was later given to the well-known women's college there.* Carry on along the road as it drops downhill, parallel to it, to reach a gate in the corner of the field. Go through the gate and along an old fenced track lined with some fine beech trees. *As the track drops down you will see how Dolgellau developed at a good crossing point of the Afon Wnion. The town's central older buildings, built of the dark grey volcanic stone and roofed with local slate, seem to fit more easily into the natural landscape than some of the later developments.*

6 Continue down to the first of the houses, and then go RIGHT and steeply downhill along another rough surfaced track. When a surfaced road is reached keep ahead, again steeply downhill, until an open area of crossroads is reached. Go ahead and slightly left and continue down to arrive at the town centre, Eldon Square.

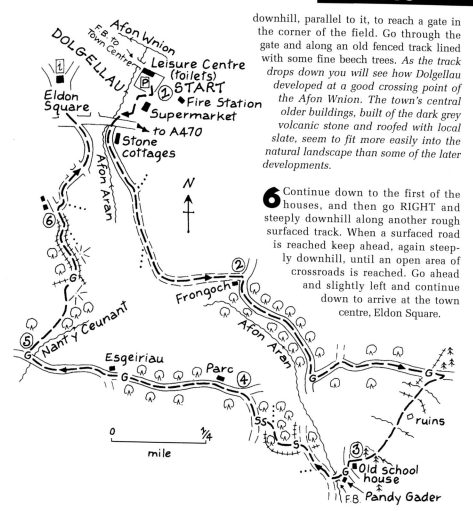

down to reach its lowest level, crossing the stream Nant y Ceunant.

5 When you reach the bridge go RIGHT through a gate along a signed wide track, with the stream below on the right. Keep along this wide green track as it moves away from the stream and rises slightly. *There are good views to the right of Mynydd Moel and soon, ahead, to Dolgellau and beyond.* When a wall ahead is approached, go RIGHT

WALK 19

LLYN Y GADAIR

DESCRIPTION A moderately energetic 4½ mile walk, mainly in open country. On the outward part, the towering cliffs of the Cadair Idris northern escarpment get closer and closer until the route reaches the lovely Llyn y Gadair, set below Cadair's high peaks. The uphill walk to the lake has some fairly steep sections, and the ¾ mile immediately before reaching the lake crosses open moorland. This section must not be undertaken in mist or very low cloud. And after heavy rain, the stream at **X** can be tricky to cross – search for the easiest point. The return from the lake is along the lower section of the well used Foxes Path and is all downhill, with fine views across the Mawddach valley. If visibility is good this is an exceptional walk for all who enjoy dramatic views. Allow 3 to 4 hours.

START National Park car park and picnic area at Ty Nant. SH 698152.

DIRECTIONS Leave Dolgellau from the top (southern) end of Eldon Square along Cadair Road towards Tywyn. After ½ mile, just before a petrol station, take the minor road half-LEFT signed Cadair Idris. The car park is 3 miles further along, on the right.

1 From the car park go back out onto the road and turn RIGHT along it. After about 100 yards, at a telephone booth, go LEFT along a wide rough surfaced track leading to *Ty Nant*. Carry on past the farm buildings through a swing gate ahead and over a footbridge. Keep on ahead along the track with a stream on the right and, later, another on the left. When a slightly more open area is reached, follow the waymark direction around to the RIGHT to go between two stone walls. Go through a swing gate – *there is a memorial tablet here* – and cross the footbridge to continue along the path with a fence on the right. An open area is soon reached. Go LEFT uphill. The path becomes stepped in places and, after about ¼ mile, reaches a gate in a wall.

2 Go through the gate and continue along the wide, green path ahead for about ¼ mile to reach another gate in a wall. Go through it and immediately cross a bridge over a small stream. Pass a ladder stile in the wall on the right, and walk on to another bridge over a small stream just 40 yards beyond the ladder stile. *DO NOT* cross this bridge but go very sharp LEFT onto a grassy mound. Look for a narrow, much less distinct, path up ahead about 12 yards from the small stream on the right, running roughly parallel to it. It goes in a south-easterly direction towards the highest point of Cyfrwy ahead. *It is important to locate this narrow track* because there are few landmarks hereabouts, but once on the track it can be followed right across this area. After about 100 yards the track curves slightly LEFT away from the stream. Keep along it, all the time going towards the near-vertical high rock escarpment and screes ahead. Cross a small stream, and when some large grassy mounds are reached the track goes slightly LEFT to avoid them. It passes about 30 yards to the right of the ruins of a shepherd's cottage. Here, carry on ahead on the track (NOT up on to the mound) as it goes to the LEFT of the low shoulder of a grass covered mound.

3 The track soon passes about 30 yards to the left of an old sheep pen, and the rock and screes at the base of Cyfrwy become fully visible. The aim now is to reach the grass covered mounds ahead, immediately to the left of the scree-covered area. When the path reaches an area completely covered with rocks go slightly LEFT across them and out to the track, now again through heather. At the base of the next grassy mound follow the track as it curves RIGHT and steeply up to the top of the mound. It goes along the ridge at the top of the mound with a mass of tangled boulders down on the right. When the ridge drops slightly, and about 30 yards before rocks covering the ridge ahead, go LEFT down and then up a grassy ridge to the left of a large hollowed out area. Carry on along the path on this ridge and when at the head of the gully on the right, follow the path slightly RIGHT as it rises up the grassy slope ahead. Look for a vertical, small, but distinctive rock at the very top of the mound ahead, appearing like an isolated miniature standing stone. Follow the path towards it. *At this rock, part of Llyn y Gadair is now visible ahead.* Carry on along the path towards the lake, down and up amongst the rocks. There are choices, but keep aiming towards the lake and it will soon be reached. *It has a wonderful setting below Penygadair (2928 ft), the highest point of the Cadair Idris range.*

4 When you must leave, go LEFT along the lake edge to the point furthest away from the crags, where the path goes down through boulders alongside the small gully made by the lake's outlet stream. Carry on down the main path. The path passes close to the left of another lake, Llyn Gafr. Cross the outlet stream and carry on along the broad path ahead. It crosses a flat area then curves left to another stream. Cross this and go immediately LEFT along its bank. After about 100 yards a wall is reached. Go through the gap in it and turn sharp LEFT to follow either of the tracks above the stream. In another 100 yards, just before a fence, the path goes to the RIGHT and then becomes a broad green track. Carry on along this, roughly parallel to the fence on the left. Cross a small stream close to the fence and keep walking down to reach a gate in a wall.

5 Go through the gate and along the path ahead. This soon passes some old cottage ruins and through a gate in the wall

ahead. The path continues ahead and crosses two streams, and then soon curves LEFT dropping down to near a wall. With this wall on the left, the path rises steeply for a short distance. Soon after dropping again, a small dwelling comes into view immediately below, and the path goes RIGHT, away from the wall. It meets another wall and *Llyn Gwernan* is soon seen ahead. Follow the path down to the hotel. At the road go LEFT to return to the car park.

39

■ Leave the car park by the swing gate close to the toilets and turn RIGHT along the wide rough surfaced track. Follow this track to reach another swing gate. Go through it and turn LEFT, passing the Visitor Centre and Café *(open 10.00-17.00)*. After crossing a bridge over a small river go RIGHT, and through a gate into a wooded area. Follow the stepped track up, and through another gate, into open countryside. Continue along the clear track, soon with a mountain stream close on the right. Follow this path upwards, generally now less steeply, as it curves left and then right into the upper valley of Cwm Cau. As the path ascends to the rim ahead, keep straight ahead, ignoring paths to the left, and go into the basin to reach the lake, Llyn Cau. *It is at a height of about 1500 feet, is about 130 feet deep and set in a fine example of a glaciated basin. This wild area is home to upland birds such as the raven and ring ouzel. The pyramid top straight ahead is the summit of Mynydd Pencoed, 2617 feet. Penygadair, the summit of Cadair Idris, is just out of sight to the right.*

2 To continue the walk, turn around from the lake and look back along the route taken to reach it. Then go half-RIGHT across the grassy area to reach the laid track going steeply up to the ridge on the right. Go up this track to the top. Turn RIGHT and follow the well worn track around this southern ridge high above Llyn Cau, eventually crossing a ladder stile to stand on the top of Mynydd Pencoed. *This is a dramatic view-*

point, encompassing Penygadair, 2928 feet, about ¾ mile to the north. The route to it is obvious and clear for those who wish to take it, and if you have the time it is a pity to miss going to the summit.

3 This walk continues from the summit of Mynydd Pencoed along the broad ridge away from Llyn Cau. Follow the broken fence south-westwards, keeping it on your left. Ignore the ladder stile in the fence after about 100 yards, and carry on to reach a low fence directly ahead, across the route being taken. Cross it by the stile and continue ahead, still keeping parallel to the fence on the left. After about ¼ mile another ladder stile is reached in this fence. Cross the stile and go down alongside a fence on the left. Go down to the small lake ahead and pass to the right of it, close to the outlying pools, and follow the faint track of the farmer's mountain vehicle. These tracks move closer to the fence after rounding the knoll behind the lake, but when the land is about to drop very steeply they turn right to take a less steep zig-zag route down. This is preferable to following the fence closely. The aim is to reach the fence and wall at the bottom of the slope, running at right angles to the fence on the left.

4 Go through the gate in the fence ahead and a gap in the wall, and follow the vehicle tracks to the right, staying on them as they take an easy route down to the next gate. Go through it and then half-LEFT down to join the rough surfaced road. Turn LEFT and keep on the road, crossing two stiles,

WALK 20
LLYN CAU, CADAIR IDRIS & TAL-Y-LLYN

DESCRIPTION A challenging and fairly strenuous 7 mile walk. It first reaches Llyn Cau, a spectacular glacial lake, closely enclosed on three sides by towering rock and scree, and then climbs above the lake to the summit of Mynydd Pencoed (2617 feet) for extensive views in all directions. From here the summit of Cadair Idris itself (2928 feet) can easily be reached. The return is by a little used but easy grassy route with fine views around the top of another cwm, to drop down to the side of the Tal-y-llyn lake. This is the most challenging walk in this book, and should not be attempted in bad weather. On a fine, clear, day it is very rewarding. Allow 5½ hours, but 7 hours if extending the walk to include the summit of Cadair Idris.

START The Dol Idris Snowdonia National Park car park at Minffordd. SH 732115.

DIRECTIONS Leave Dolgellau on the A470 towards Machynlleth, turning RIGHT along the A487 at the Cross Foxes Inn, 3 miles out of the town. After a further 4 miles turn RIGHT along the B4405, signed Tywyn, and almost immediately turn RIGHT again into the car park.

to the farm *Rhiwogof* below. At the farm approach, cross the stile in the fence ahead and go LEFT alongside the fence.

5 Go through the gate ahead and continue along the track, which soon drops down into the steep-sided valley containing the stream flowing swiftly out of Cwm Amarch. Turn RIGHT along the fence above the stream and then, near the bottom of the field, go LEFT through a gate. Cross the stream by the footbridge and go through the gate ahead. Follow the track down to the surfaced road.

6 Turn LEFT and follow this minor road which, after four gates and a footbridge alongside a ford, joins the B4405. Go ahead along it to return to the car park.

WELSH

The meanings of some of the common words found in local place names

aber	mouth	**foel**	bare hill	**newydd**	new
afon	river, stream	**fynydd**	mountain	**ogof**	cave
allt	hillside	**garth**	enclosure, hill	**pandy**	mill
bach	small	**glas**	green, blue	**pant**	hollow
banc	hill			**parc**	field, park
blaen	head of valley	**glyder**	heap	**pen**	top
bont	bridge	**glyn**	glen	**penmaen**	rocky headland
bryn	hill	**gors**	bog	**pistyll**	waterfall, spout
bwlch	pass	**grug**	heather		
		gwen	white	**plas**	mansion
cadair (cader)	chair	**gyrn**	peak	**porth**	port
caer	fort			**pwll**	pool
capel	chapel	**hafod**	summer dwelling		
castell	castle	**hen**	old	**rhaeadr**	waterfall
cefn	ridge	**hendre**	winter dwelling	**rhiw**	hill
ceunant	ravine			**rhos**	marsh, moor
coch	red	**heol**	road		
coed	wood	**hir**	long	**rhyd**	ford
craig	rock				
croes	cross	**isaf**	lowest	**sarn**	road
cwm	valley			**sych**	dry
		llan	church		
dinas	fort, city	**llech**	slate	**tarren**	hill
dol	meadow	**llidiart**	gate	**tomen**	mound
du	black	**llwyd**	grey	**traeth**	shore, beach
dwr	water	**llyn**	lake		
dyffryn	valley			**traws**	across
		maen	stone	**tref**	hamlet, home
eglwys	church	**maes**	field		
esgair	hillspur	**mawr**	big	**twll**	hole
		melin	mill	**ty**	house
fach	small	**moch**	pigs		
fan	high place	**moel**	bare hill	**uchaf**	highest
fawr	large	**mor**	sea		
fechan	small	**mynach**	monk	**y, yr**	the, of the
felin	mill	**mynydd**	mountain	**ynys**	island
ffordd	road			**ysgol**	school
ffynnon	spring, well	**nant**	stream	**ystrad**	valley floor
		neuadd	hall		